Time of Strength

14 Words of Encouragement for Parents of Children with Special Needs

Janis C. Jones

365 Words of Encouragement Media Group provides devotional books and products which are available at special quantity discounts for bulk purchases for sales promotions, premiums, fundraising, and educational needs. For details, visit our website www.encouragedevotions.com.

A Time of Strength, 14 Words of Encouragement for Parents of Children with Special Needs
Published by 365 Words of Encouragement Media Group
Devotions Department
151 Highway 74 South, #2272
Peachtree City, GA 30269
www.encouragedevotions.com

Written by Janis C. Jones
www.janiscjones.com

Dedication

To the most beautiful girl in the world, Daya - an artist, writer and overcomer of every challenge she ever faces!

For Parents

This book is for you if . . .

- You just received a diagnosis for your child and are overwhelmed. You don't know where to turn for advice or information.

- You have tried everything you know to do (every medication, therapy, doctor and treatment). Maybe it is working or maybe not. Either way, you find yourself scared and unsure of your child's future.

- You find that you are in a place of uncertainty and you just need to be encouraged.

Table of Contents

Why Encouragement Matters

When listening to perspectives regarding children with special needs, it is often very limiting. The conversation usually focuses on what a child cannot do or cannot become. To combat that perspective, there must be a redirection of the conversation toward the truth of who your child was created to be and a great expectation for who they will become. It is about believing in the best, living the best and loving your way through it all with your child.

This devotional book was developed from inspiration found in Ecclesiastes 3:1 which says, "*To everything there is a season, and a time to every purpose under the heaven:*" There is truly a "time" and "season" for everything, especially in parenting a special needs child. There are times of grief, confusion and sadness. However, there are also times of new adventures, excitement and joy. Though all parents live through similar "seasons" in raising their children, they are experienced in different ways that are unique when you parent a child with special needs. Others may not understand those differences, and this often leads to parents feeling isolated and discouraged.

At 365 Words of Encouragement Media Group, our devotional books are designed to stand in faith with you and your child to overcome whatever challenges they may face. We will walk with you through each **"Time"** of parenting. No matter what difficulty you are facing, you can find your specific area of need and receive encouragement. This book is here to make a positive change in your life!

Empowerment for Parents

Encouragement is empowerment. We want to elevate your heart and mind to a place of hope and joy. Our goal is to equip you with spiritual and practical tools that will serve to enhance and promote successful parenting.

"Time of Strength" is the first in a series of devotionals that will cover different aspects of parenting a child with special needs. In this book, we focus on staying strong in your spirit, soul and body. For those times of physical and mental exhaustion, this book will encourage you with promises from God's word and provide you with a step-by-step action plan to regain and sustain your strength. We have also included scripture cards for you to cut out and carry with you or post on your wall.

There are 14 aspects of walking in strength that are addressed. Each area is explained through a devotion that provides insight into the meaning of a scripture. There is also an action plan that includes practical steps to help increase your strength in that area. You can go as fast or as slow as you need. There is no time requirement. You can take one devotion each day or one devotion each week. The book is designed to fit your own individual pace.

Through our partnership with the charitable organization Encourage 365, Inc., we offer free online empowerment sessions where we discuss each devotion and action plan. Visit encourage365.org to sign-up and participate.

Thank you for allowing us this opportunity to share the joy of God's word with you. We believe that you will experience a great transformation and elevation in your parenting. We are excited to be on the journey with you for your child's success.

Time to Believe

With every season of life, there is a time to believe the best for your child

Real Encouragement

At 365 Words of Encouragement, one thing we know is that true encouragement is found in the word of God. If you want to be encouraged on the journey of healing with your child, consider God's word. It will work for you if you are willing to believe it and apply it to your life.

What we want to do is share with you what we know to be true. It is an undying, never failing, unconditional love that will empower you to overcome any challenge you ever face in life. We want to introduce you to Jesus. Know this:

1. <u>Jesus loves you.</u> No matter what you have done, He gave His life for you so that you don't have to bear any guilt or shame. He died for your past, present and future, to remove everywhere you missed the mark and He replaced it with His love and grace. *John 3:16*

2. <u>If you confess with our mouth and believe in your heart that Jesus is Lord, you shall be saved</u>. "Saved from what?" you may ask. Saved from defeat – that is defeat in this world and in the time to come; defeat over spiritual deadness; defeat over bondage; defeat over fear; defeat over the destruction of your soul. *Romans 10:9, Luke 7:21-22*

3. <u>There is a better way to live.</u> Accepting Jesus into your life brings unspeakable joy and peace that no person can fully express in just words on a page. It is an overwhelming love that will have a positive effect on every area of your life, including parenting.

To receive victory and a life with Jesus Christ, say this aloud:

"Heavenly Father, I believe that Jesus is your son. You sent Him to pay the price for my sin. I believe you raised Him from the dead and He is Lord. Jesus, come into my life. I receive you as Lord of my life now and forever more. In Jesus name, Amen."

Praise God! Welcome to the family of Christ. You have just received the greatest gift of love and grace. This book will help show you the tools needed to set you on a course for victorious parenting of your precious child. As you move forward in life, be sure to get connected to a good, bible- based church. Read the bible and stay encouraged!

If you don't have a bible and are unable to download a bible app on your mobile device, go to encourage365.org to get information on receiving a free bible and other resources.

Action Plan

Now that you have taken the step toward a life of encouragement through God's word, it is good to set out your next steps to keep moving towards a new outlook for your child.

STEP 1: Get a bible –Today, technology has made the bible available at our fingertips. You can find various versions of the bible in just about any language of the world. Whether you use a bible app on your mobile device or download a digital copy to a computer or book reader, the word of God has the same powerful effect. Of course, if you are not comfortable with technology or live in an area where you do not have easy access to technology, you can always rely on the standard book. Afterall, it has survived for thousands of years and it will outlast the technology age too!

STEP 2: Get connected – Creating a community of encouragement for yourself is vital. Look for opportunities to intentionally build relationships with others. That includes connecting with a church or ministry. It also involves reaching out to organizations that can assist with supporting you and your child.

STEP 3: Stay Encouraged – Make encouragement a part of your regular self-care routine. Be sure to take a moment to read a scripture each day. In addition, the charitable organization Encourage 365, Inc. dedicates itself to providing encouragement resources and services to parents of children with special needs. Visit encourage365.org and sign-up to receive weekly encouragement information, register for a newsletter and join the encouragement community.

What specific actions will you take to make encouragement a priority in your life?

1. _____
2. _____
3. _____

Prayer:

Lord, thank you for leading me to a better place of peace by receiving encouragement from your word. Help me on this path to finding greater strength in you.

Daily Declaration:

My greatest encouragement comes directly from the word of God.

* If you do not have a bible and are unable to download a bible app to your mobile device, go to encourage365.com to get information on receiving a free bible and other resources.

Time of Strength

*Numbers 13:30, "And Caleb stilled the people before Moses, and said, Let us go up at once, and possess it; **for we are well able to overcome it**"*
(KJV)

You Are an Overcomer!

There are so many things that come your way when you have a child with special needs. Your days are filled with constant tasks from traveling back and forth to see doctors, dealing with sudden emergencies, spending late nights seeking answers and researching treatments over the internet. It can really become overwhelming! You find yourself wondering if you have the strength to handle it all.

One place to gain insight for strength is to look at Caleb in Numbers 13:30. Caleb was determined to secure a new land for God's people. Yet, the territory they were to enter was full of GIANTS! Those "GIANTS" represented obstacles that were so great it looked as if it was impossible to conquer them. Even though Caleb knew there were challenges ahead of him, he stood before everyone and said, "Let us go up at once, and possess it; **for we are well able to overcome it**".

To make that statement, Caleb had an inner resolve that was unwavering. He had to know something about God's strength operating in his life. He had to know that God was with him, that God had equipped him for the journey and that God had given him everything needed to go forward and accomplish the task. That same idea and resolve applies to you in your parenting. Know that God's strength is operating in you, equipping you and providing everything you need to be exactly what your child needs.

Having confidence in God's strength is important. His strength is working in your life every day. Just like Caleb, no matter how challenging things may be at any given time, you were created, designed and equipped to overcome it. You are not alone - God's strength is with you. You **ARE** an overcomer!

Action Plan

STEP 1: Reflect - Look at the full scripture of Numbers 13:30. Before Caleb made the declaration of being an overcomer, he first quieted the crowd so they could listen. Take a moment and quiet your mind. Sit still and reflect on the true nature of God's strength as being powerful, unmovable and triumphant. Envision and embrace that same level of strength operating in you.

STEP 2: Identify - What are the areas that look impossible to you right now? It may be a concern with your child's diagnosis or challenges with your child's school. Be specific and write it down.

_____

_____

_____

_____

STEP 3: Address: Begin to pray over each area you identified above. Allow God to speak to your heart about the matter. Write down one (1) action that you will take as a stand of strength to address each area. It may be to begin researching the issue to gain more understanding or find an organization in your area that can provide support or advocacy services.

_____

_____

_____

_____

Prayer:

Lord help me recognize and take hold of your strength that is working in my life today. Show me ways to stand in your strength to confront any difficult situations, no matter how great the challenge may seem.

Daily Declaration:

God's strength is operating in my life. I **AM** an overcomer!

Nehemiah 8:10, "**Go home and prepare a feast, holiday food and drink; and share it with those who don't have anything:** This day is holy to God. Don't feel bad. **The joy of God is your strength!**" (MSG)

Embrace Joy . . . and share it too

It's a good thing to have fun! Sometimes we get so focused on everyday responsibilities that we never enjoy the goodness of living life. Regardless of the nature of your child's special needs, you are blessed. You are living, breathing and ready to experience another day of God's grace. It is time to embrace joy.

Nehemiah 8:10 says, "the joy of God is your strength". Contained within the concept of joy is the ability to be strong. Joy is something different than mere happiness. You can become happy when events and circumstances are good and favorable. However, joy is an ability to experience delight and pleasure, even when circumstances are negative or overwhelming. There is an inner strength that God provides for you that enables you to enjoy the fullness of life, no matter what conditions you may face.

Regardless of the situations and circumstances that come with raising a child with special needs, there is no reason you can't enjoy yourself throughout your parenting journey. You can sing a song as you rise in the morning, explore a new route as you drive to your destination, take a bite of your favorite food or just take a moment to sit and listen to the birds (even if it is just for one minute). Take time to enjoy yourself.

Once you've done that, you are now able to go and share that enjoyment with others. You can be a vessel that God uses to bring enjoyment to other parents. It is good to encourage and support one another. Look at Nehemiah 8:10 again. In this scripture, people who were celebrating for themselves were also instructed to "share it with those who don't have anything". Sharing joy with others provides strength – for both you and the other person. You can try this in very simple ways such as calling another parent to encourage them. You can also share things such as books, therapy materials, and beautiful things like flowers. Be a blessing. Embracing the enjoyment of life and showing love to others will result in abounding strength for all.

Helpful Hint for Sharing Joy

Cut out the scripture cards on pages 73-88. You can make copies and give a set to another parent to help them stay encouraged.

Action Plan

STEP 1: Reflect – Take an honest review of how you see your everyday life and circumstances. Are you finding yourself bogged down with the same routines and busy schedules? Are you enjoying your days to the fullest? Be honest with where you are right now.

_____

_____

_____

_____

STEP 2: Pray - Take a moment and talk to God about your life. Prayer does not have to be a formal set of rules or processes. You can simply talk to Him like you would your best friend and ask for help. Be honest, open and be in expectation to receive guidance.

STEP 3: Embrace – After prayer, be open to taking a different approach to your day. Write down three (3) things you will do this next week differently to experience and share joy. Think about the things you like, desire or are curious about and take a step toward experiencing those things. For example, if you like to laugh, look for a free Podcast of your favorite comedian and listen while you go through your daily schedule. If you like perfume or nice smells around you, but you don't have the resources to purchase something new, see if you can get some free samples of fragrances (some may even be offered online). You can also share samples with other parents who may struggle with finding joy. Money, or the lack thereof, does not have to determine your ability to experience or share joy.

Be open to thinking outside of the box. Write your new action steps below.

1. _____
2. _____
3. _____

Prayer:

Thank you God for equipping me with joy to walk out my journey as a parent. Help me each day to embrace areas of joy and receive strength to live and parent effectively for myself, my child and those engaged in our lives.

Daily Declaration:

Today and every day, I walk in the joy of the Lord. I embrace joy and I share joy – for the joy of God is my strength.

Luke 6:38, "**_Give and it shall be given unto you; good measure pressed down and shaken together, and running over shall men give into your bosom._** *For with the same measure that you meet withal it shall be measured to you again.*" *(KJV)*

The Seed of Strength

Fatigue is a real concern for parents of children with special needs. This occurs when your body is exhausted, sleep deprived and unable to function at its best. It can also be mental, where you are emotionally sensitive and you begin struggling with anger, sadness or fear. For some parents, it becomes a time of desperation where there is a need to cry out for help.

It is during these moments, where God's grace is experienced the most. It is when your phone rings and someone calls with an encouraging word just when you need it. Or, you receive a text message that reminds you of how special you are. It may even be an encouraging testimony you hear that makes you smile. These are things that give us supernatural strength to go on. They are times of encouragement that serve as seeds of strength planted in our lives. These "seeds" grow on the inside of our hearts and carry us through even the worst of times.

One thing about seeds, as they grow, they produce fruits that have even more seeds. Think about that for a moment. A seed planted eventually yields more seeds which allows for even more people to enjoy the fruit produced. When you are a parent who has received God's grace to be strengthened by the love of another, you can also take steps to be a giver of strength as well. You can send out messages to other parents to say "just thinking of you" or share stories of healing. You can plant the seed of strength.

Luke 6:38 reminds us that as we give, it shall also be given back into our life in "good measure" that is "pressed down, shaken together and running over". Many times, you will hear this scripture when others refer to financial giving such as donations to a church or organization. But the concept of "giving" is much greater. The seeds of strength we give to others are also the seeds for strength we receive. In other words, as you become one who is a giver of encouragement to strengthen others, God's divine provision to experience the fullness of his supernatural strength is expanded for you as well. The strength and encouragement you need as a parent is connected to the strength and encouragement you give.

Helpful Hint for Growing your
Seed of Strength

Sometimes the greatest source of strength is just being heard. Having a willingness to listen to hear the true heart of another not only allows for them to be strengthened, but you also. Becoming a good listener is a great attribute and can make you stronger as you approach difficult situations.

Action Plan

STEP 1: Imagine – Envision the process of a seed that is planted and then produces fruit. For example, the seed of one mango can yield a tree that produces 50 more mangos, each carrying one new seed. That is 50 new seeds coming from just one seed! Think about that in the context of encouragement and how one act of encouragement to strengthen someone can produce many more actions of strength for yourself and others as well.

STEP 2: Review - Review the entire verse in Luke 6:38 several times with the mindset of seed planting that you just envisioned. What would it look like to experience a seed that is multiplied so greatly that it comes to you in "good measure, pressed down and shaken together, and running over". We gave the example of one seed producing 50 seeds. Luke 6:38 describes something even greater than that - "pressed down, shaken together and running over"! What new understanding have you gained from this scripture when considering encouragement and strength for yourself and others.

STEP 3: Give – What are ways in which you can encourage and strengthen other parents of children with special needs? It does not need to be anything that requires a lot of planning or take a large amount of time. It could be as simple as a text message of encouragement or a post on social media that strengthens the heart and soul of others. Ask God to show you specific ways to give the seed of strength.

_____

_____

_____

_____

Prayer:

Lord teach me how to be mindful of giving strength to others. Create in me a heart that encourages others in moments of weakness. I thank you now for the strength that I receive from seeds of encouragement.

Daily Declaration:

As I strengthen and encourage others, I too am strengthened and encouraged! I receive God's abundance of strength in good measure that is pressed down, shaken together and running over.

*Philippians 4:13, "I can do **all things through Christ, who strengthens me**." (EHV)*

It's Not on You

Difficult situations in life never come at convenient times. In the midst of dealing with issues like divorce and financial struggles, parents of children with special needs have additional challenges they must confront.

To overcome these situations, it is important to know that the strength to endure against pressure is not something that you can just come up with on your own. True strength only comes from God. Philippians 4:13 says, "I can do all things through Christ who strengthens me". Relying on God is the key to victory. It is not on you to be perfect or flawless. Jesus is the only one who lived the perfect life. The amazing strength He showed on the cross is unmatched. He carried all of our sins, forgave us, loved us and provided everlasting, abundant life for us. You do not have to try to operate with that kind of strength because Jesus has already done that for you.

Trusting God and relying on the strength that only His grace provides enables you to be at peace. That means you can address any challenge or task that comes before you, knowing that God's strength is working in you. So, rest your heart and mind. It's not on you. Remove the pressure from yourself and put your trust in God.

Action Plan

STEP 1: Meditate – Spend time reading and thinking about the scripture Philippians 4:13. Speak it out loud several times and boldly say, "I can do all things through Christ, who strengthens me". Even if you have to say it through tears, it's okay. Allow that scripture to get into your heart and mind. Allow yourself to believe it.

STEP 2: Reveal - Sit quietly for a moment and begin to uncover those areas where you are trying to do it all in your own strength. These are usually those areas where you find yourself struggling the most. Don't be afraid to be honest with yourself. It can be anything from a task you are trying to complete to an attitude you have that has become negative and unmanageable. Remember, God is here to help.

_____

_____

_____

_____

STEP 3: Release– Now that these areas have been revealed, it is time to let go. Remember, it's not on you. It is God's strength within you that you can rely upon. Begin today by committing to a new approach. Write a personal statement for yourself where you commit to applying God's strength to those situations where you are trying to do it on your own. Here is an example. If you are struggling with organizing a peaceful, daily schedule. You could write:

"Lord I thank you for helping me with my daily schedule. I rest and rely on your strength as I set out to organize and provide for my child today. I will not be distraught, anxious or depressed about this daily schedule. I know your strength is greater than mine and I trust you instead of myself. I know that I can do all things through you who strengthens me."

Write your personal statement for the areas revealed to you:

_____
_____
_____
_____

Prayer:

Thank you Lord for strengthening me. Help me as I begin to learn how to rely on your abounding strength each day.

Daily Declaration:

God's strength is greater than my own. I confront every challenge knowing that God's strength empowers me. Today and every day, I do all things through Christ who strengthens me.

*1 John 4:4, "But you belong to God, my dear children. **You have already won a victory** over those people, **because the Spirit who lives in you is greater than the spirit who lives in the world.**"* (NLT)

Greater is in You

For parents of children with special needs, there is always pressure to find the appropriate medical services or identify the right school. There is an ever-present concern to always make the right decisions. Stress can begin to bear down upon your heart, mind and body. Over time, it can drain you.

Fortunately, God reminds us of a tremendous gift we have been given. It is the gift of Himself living inside our heart. The truth is, what you have living on the inside of you is actually greater than anything outside of you. God Himself, is working in you to comfort you, strengthen you, love you and assure you are equipped to deal with whatever comes your way. According to 1 John 4:4, you have already won the victory, "because the Spirit who lives in you is greater than the spirit who lives in the world." That means, whatever stressors of life you experience, you win over them because they will never be greater or more powerful than God who lives inside your heart.

When you need strength, remind yourself of the greatness within. Nothing on this earth will ever be greater than what you have on the inside. The greatest strength of all, God Himself, is living in you and He is there to strengthen you right now.

Action Plan

STEP 1: Have Fun – Think of what it was like when you were a child and you believed in superheroes. Though a character had one human persona in everyday life, when trouble emerged, they transformed into this being that could leap over tall buildings, fly in the air or have extraordinary strength. They were able to do these things due to the supernatural characteristics that existed within. That same principle applies to you. While living your everyday human life, you possess God's supernatural strength. With God, you become a superhero - able to supernaturally handle any issue your child may face. Take a moment to have some fun imagining yourself as a superhero. Envision yourself using God's power within you to overcome negative comments in one leap, knock down obstacles hindering your child's access to medical services and flying high above any labels or limited expectations others want to have for your child. Enjoy yourself. Take pleasure in looking at yourself in a new way.

STEP 2: Get Excited - You have a new vision for yourself. You are not a weak or helpless parent. You are empowered by God living within you. Smile about it and let joy arise in your heart. Read 1 John 4:4 again out loud. Write down how you feel about yourself now. How has your view of yourself and your ability to be strengthened as a parent changed?

_____

_____

_____

_____

STEP 3: Activate – It is now time to put the new you into action. Identify areas of your parenting where you previously saw an issue as enormous or just too much for you to handle. Take the scripture in 1 John 4:4 along with the new vision of yourself and write out a new strategy to address the problem (such as contacting a different service provider or researching alternative options). Make sure to pray first and ask God to help you with a new plan of action. Whatever the approach, always be loving and kind. Remember, it is God who is within you; therefore, your approach should reflect the nature of God as well.

_____
_____
_____
_____

Prayer:

Lord, help me to see myself differently by embracing the goodness and greatness of your strength within me. Give me new ideas and perspectives on how to approach challenges with parenting.

Daily Declaration:

God's strength within me is greater than anything outside of me. It is with his strength that I stand equipped and ready to have the victory over any challenge I face.

*Ephesians 3:16, "That He would grant you, according to the **riches of His glory** to be **strengthened with might** by His Spirit in the inner man."* (KJV)

Mighty Strength

Strength comes in different levels. You can see this when observing small ants. They can lift up to 50 times their body weight. As humans, if we could lift just 20 times our body weight, that would be about 4,000 pounds. That is the equivalent of a midsize vehicle. Imagine that! If your car stopped working, you could just carry it to the repair shop! Clearly the ant is embodied with a different level of physical strength. What kind of strength has God placed within you?

It is important to understand the full nature of strength that dwells inside of you. Ephesians 3:16 states that according to the richness of God's glory, He has granted you to be "strengthened with *might* in your inner man". The strength you have been given is not a little zap of strength or some small portion of strength. It is a strength that is richly supplied – a *MIGHTY* strength! The bible defines the word "might" as an inherent power that has great influence and has the ability to perform miracles. It is a strength that will never waver or decrease. It will endure and is able to outlast any circumstances, no matter how difficult.

What exciting news! At this very moment, you have a mighty strength that has been freely given to you by God. You don't have to work hard to make strength appear in your life. You can trust what God has already given you to handle whatever needs to be done with confident assurance. God's strength will carry you through. Declare this today, "I am strengthened with might in my inner man. I have an abundant supply of strength. I can trust and peacefully rely on all God has given me."

Action Plan

STEP 1: Observe – Learn from the ants! Yes, spend a few minutes looking at the ants and their strength. You can find many quick videos through an online search on your computer or mobile device. Though it may sound a little silly to you now, try it anyway. You will be surprised what insight you will receive. Consider how God equipped them with an internal strength for them to do whatever they are purposed to do at that moment. Write down your thoughts.

_____

_____

_____

_____

STEP 2: Internalize - God has equipped you with "mighty" strength. It may not be displayed as supernatural physical strength (though it can be), but rather an internal resolve - a purpose and determination to handle whatever challenge is present in your life. How do you see God's mighty strength working in your life?

_____

_____

_____

_____

STEP 3: Speak – Make a promise that whenever you are in a moment of weakness or feeling discouraged, you will appeal to God's mighty strength within you and repeat the scripture. Take the verse from Ephesians 1:3 and read it out loud. Cut out the scripture card on page 79 and keep it in your pocket. You can also try attaching it to your mirror. Whatever you need to do to remind and encourage yourself when you feel vulnerable, **DO IT!** Get radical with it! Speak the word in the face of opposition.

Prayer:

Lord help me to be mindful of your mighty strength. As I approach this day, I take hold of your steadfast power, resolve and influence. I move forward today beyond any distractions and difficulties, knowing that your mighty strength has prepared and equipped me.

Daily Declaration:

As I face this day, I am focused on God's "MIGHTY" strength given to me to address every situation and circumstance.

*Genesis 22:17, "That **in blessing I will bless thee, and in multiplying I will multiply thy seed** as the stars of heaven, and the sand which is upon the sea shore; and thy seed shall possess the gate of his enemies"* (KJV)

Multiplied Strength

God's promises are wonderful guarantees where we can expect miracles to happen in our lives. One great promise can be seen in the life of Abraham. In Genesis 22:17, God tells Abraham that "in blessing I will bless thee, and in *multiplying* I will *multiply* thy seed". Imagine that - a promise of multiplication!

In looking through Abrahams' life, we can see where God fulfilled His promise. Abraham experienced great multiplication with his children. He was described as having descendants as numerous as the stars (Hebrews 11:12 *(BSB)*). He possessed a multiplied level resources becoming *"extremely wealthy in livestock and silver and gold"*. (Genesis 13:2 *(BSB)*). He even experienced multiplication far into his life when he was "old and well along in years" (Genesis 24:1 *(BSB)*). Everything in Abraham's life was impacted by God's promise. It was supernatural multiplication.

Just as Abraham received multiplied results of God's goodness in his life, you can expect that promise to be extended to you in your parenting. You can view all things from a multiplied perspective, including your strength, time, energy and resources. If you have been caring for your child all day only to find yourself tired and in need of strength, take a moment to reflect on God's promise of multiplication. Picture yourself being increased, impacted and enlarged by God's supernatural power and strength. See yourself resilient, steadfast and living in God's promise of multiplication.

Action Plan

STEP 1: Remember – Think back to a time as a young child when time would seem to last forever. School days seemed to be an eternity. Yet as we got older, days seemed to get shorter and faster. Why? It is the same 24 hours in every day. Could it be a difference in perspective? When we are young, we think of each day as endless. There is an innocent hopefulness about the daily events and activities, even if they don't go just as planned. It was just the way you approached the day. Yet becoming older, many times the day is not faced with joyful expectation. Instead, there is often dread, regret and concern that you will not have enough time to get things done. One is an expectation of abundant time and opportunity, while the other is an expectation of limitation and insufficiency. Spend a few minutes thinking about your favorite childhood days - those days that just seemed endless. Allow yourself to be flooded with the joy of that time and what it felt like to be hopeful in anticipation for your day.

STEP 2: Change – It is now time to consider a change of perspective. The multiplied strength of God is available to you. Consider looking at your day with an expectation of multiplied time, strength, and resources. You probably have more available to assist you than you ever imagined. Take time to ask God to reveal to you areas of multiplication that you may not have considered before.

_____
_____
_____
_____

STEP 3: Approach – Review your daily schedule and take a new approach. There may be some areas that need to be removed from your routine. There may be better and more efficient ways of getting some things accomplished. Let God speak to you to show you areas where you have been multiplied. You do not have to accept being overwhelmed and burdened. God's multiplied strength is here for you. Write out ideas God has given you to take a new abundant, "multiplied" approach to your day.

_____

_____

_____

_____

Prayer:

Thank you Lord for helping me change my perspective. Help me to approach my day in a new way to see the multiplied blessing of strength in my life.

Daily Declaration:

As I face this day, I am focused on God's "MIGHTY" strength given to me to address every situation and circumstance.

3 John 2, "Beloved, I pray that in every way you may **_succeed and prosper and be in good health [physically], just as [I know] your soul prospers [spiritually]_**" (AMP)

Strong Body

Many parents of children with special needs struggle with their own health concerns. The daily pressures of limited time and resources create challenges with parents making their own physical health a priority. Eventually, it becomes the normal routine to put their own health in last place while everything else takes priority. This is not God's plan.

In looking at 3 John 2, it says "Beloved, I pray that in every way you may succeed and prosper and be in good health [physically], just as [I know] your soul prospers [spiritually]." It is important to recognize that as you pursue strength in your spiritual life, you must also pursue it in your physical body. You will find it difficult to operate at the fullest measure of strength unless you are willing to address the condition of your own health.

Ask yourself, "Are the foods that I eat working toward a goal of growing strength in my body?" "Am I engaging in activities that support and enhance my physical ability to care for my child?" Take an honest look at your life and evaluate your habits. Are you doing things to promote health and strength in your body? If not, God is ready to help. Pray and ask God about ways to improve your physical health. His wisdom can guide you to new and better ways to eat and live within the time and resources that you have available. Remember, a healthy body will help you be stronger and better prepared to parent your beautiful child.

Action Plan

STEP 1: Prioritize - Is your physical health a priority? Consider your weekly routine. Are you setting aside a moment of time or taking some actions that will help to renew your physical strength? Evaluate your current priorities. Where does your physical health fall in the line of priorities for your life?

_____

_____

_____

_____

STEP 2: Be Aware – What is the current status of your health? Are you up to date on your annual physical check-ups and dental visits? What concerns do you have regarding your physical health?

_____

_____

_____

_____

Step 3: Respond – What are three (3) things you can do this week to begin addressing any health concerns and improving the current state of your physical body?

1. _____

2. _____

3. _____

Prayer:

Lord, it is my desire to prioritize my physical health. Reveal to me the ways in which I can adjust my schedule, activities, nutrition and rest for my physical strength to be maximized. Thank you for helping me through this process.

Daily Declaration:

I prosper daily in my physical health. I receive God's wisdom and help to bring increased strength to every aspect of my body.

Proverbs 13:4, "...__the desires of the diligent are fully satisfied.__" (NIV)

Overcoming the "Whatever"

As situations become overwhelming, parents can enter into various types of survival mode. One of those tactics of survival is known as the *"Whatever"* attitude. It is where you become so physically tired and empty that you sit back and just let things happen. It may be that financially things start to crumble around you or you take on an "I don't care" perspective toward the responsibilities you face. When you get to this place, the biggest result is missed opportunities.

Proverbs 13:4 says, "the desires of the diligent are fully satisfied." Though you may just want to give up, there are still many opportunities coming your way. If it is money you need for a certain program or activity, there may be a scholarship or grant opportunity available. If there is a specialized medical procedure needed, there may be an opportunity for care through a university research hospital or other facility. Whatever the need, God is there to provide a solution.

Staying in expectation to diligently seek God's wisdom will open your eyes to more possibilities. Instead of being limited to just accepting whatever happens, we are able overcome the *"Whatever"* attitude and receive God's grace to show us what we need, where to go and how to obtain it. No matter what, we seize opportunities to keep moving forward.

Action Plan

STEP 1: Recognize – Sometimes, the hardest step to take is that first step of acknowledging that there is an issue that needs to be addressed. Are there areas in your parenting where you have stopped pressing forward or you are no longer believing that things can change? Have you taken on the "Whatever" attitude? Be forthcoming and open to recognize where you may have entered into this mind-set.

_____

_____

_____

_____

STEP 2: Energize – Get encouraged by God's word. It's time to fuel your spiritual tank and get reinvigorated with the promises of God. Take time today to explore and review scriptures concerning the issues you listed in Step 1. You can start with the concordance in the back of your bible to look up certain key words that will lead you to scriptures. You can also search on a bible app that will allow you to find scriptures by entering specific words. This process will bring you to specific bible verses that will help to encourage and strengthen you. List your scriptures below:

1. _____

2. _____

3. _____

STEP 3: Address – Now it's time to move forward and believe again. Take time to pray over your scriptures in Step 2. Be willing to do some new things and have a new perspective about those areas. It is okay to be nervous and cautious – just keep moving forward. Being diligent is being consistent. Even if you are taking small steps in believing differently, those steps will eventually lead you to a better place in parenting with your child.

Prayer:

Lord, thank you for loving me as a parent and encouraging me to keep believing the best for my child. In times where I may be stagnant, help me to keep moving forward. Thank you for honoring every step I take - whether it be big or small, your love propels me forward.

Daily Declaration:

I stand today embracing God's love, diligently receiving his promises and moving forward for my child.

*Genesis 2:2, "And on the seventh day **<u>God ended his work</u>** which he had made; **<u>and he rested on the seventh day from all his work which he had made</u>**."* (KJV)

It's on!

Do you ever feel like you have to be "ON" all the time as a parent? Even when you are tired, angry or sad, you have a big smile on your face, looking like you have everything together. You are there to save the day! However, in your heart, you know that you are barely hanging on. You're stressed out, frustrated and on the edge of a breakdown. It is at this moment where everything must stop and you must consider rest.

Genesis 2:2 says that God "rested on the seventh day from all His work which He had made." Rest is biblical. Our great God who created heaven and earth took time to rest. You need rest also. That means carving out time in your schedule to get sufficient sleep. It also means taking time during the week to read an article or do something relaxing.

Spiritual renewal is also a part of rest. Taking time to pray and focus on God's word is a vital part of life. As you set aside time to renew your spirit and body, you will have more strength to face all the challenges of your day. You will also be able to deal with the feelings of constantly being "on". You'll realize that God is the one who is always "on", so why do you need to be? He's got your back! Take time to rest and experience the freedom to be renewed, refreshed and recharged for another day.

Action Plan

STEP 1: Get Real – During those times when you are "ON" for everyone else, there is one person who knows the truth about where you really are - God knows. You don't have to fake it with God. You can bare your true self before your heavenly father. He will love you and accept you right where you are. Find a quiet place (even if it is sitting in your car by yourself away from the chaos of your home). Have a moment to talk with God. Reveal your heart to him and release your concerns. Get real and freely speak about where you are.

STEP 2: Revive – Read Genesis 1 (verses 1 –31) and Genesis 2:1-2. Look at what God did in creating the earth, plants, animals and humans. He took time to look over every aspect of his work and he declared it to be good. Taking time to reflect and see the goodness in all you do as a parent helps to keep you revived. There is no need to pretend to be "ON" when you are okay with who you are, what you do as a parent, and the goodness of what you are producing in your child. Take a moment to reflect on all you do for your child and acknowledge the goodness of what God is producing through you.

_____

_____

_____

_____

STEP 3: Rest – When you start the process of integrating rest into your life, the first thing to understand is that rest is intentional. You must make time for it. It is not something others can manage for you. Your spiritual and physical wellbeing are things you must govern and protect for yourself. Consider your schedule. How can you integrate time for quality periods of rest (i.e., an additional hour of sleep,10 minutes of mediation, listening to a 5-minute scripture devotion)? List ways you will intentionally seek to rest.

1. _____
2. _____
3. _____

Prayer:

Thank you, Lord, for accepting me for who I am and loving me right where you find me today. Teach me how to rest. Lead and guide me to better ways that I can rest my body and be renewed spiritually.

Daily Declaration:

I love who God made me to be and I purpose in my heart to get sufficient rest each day.

*Psalm 103:5, "Who **satisfies your mouth with good things**; so that **your youth is renewed like eagles**" (NKJV)*

Youthful Strength

The physical demands of caring for a child with special needs can be excruciating. It requires a great level of physical strength and stamina. For many parents this is challenging. It is more than just an issue of conditioning. There is also mental strain as well – a constant wondering of how long your body will be able to last to provide what your child needs.

Fortunately, the bible provides a promise to us concerning our bodies. Psalms 103:5 talks about the youthful renewal of your physical body. It says that God "satisfies your mouth with good things; so that your *youth is renewed like eagles*." That includes youthful energy, strength, endurance and even appearance. Imagine that! You can have an expectation to get stronger as your child grows older instead of dreading becoming weaker.

The starting point begins by allowing God to "satisfy your mouth with good things". Those *"good things"* are not just talking about the food you eat but also are referring to the words you speak. It is speaking words to declare God's promises, giving thanks for everything you have in life and giving praise for every accomplishment your child attains (no matter how small). How you choose to speak about your life can change your outlook, even to the point of renewing your physical body. Though good words are not a replacement for exercise, rest and healthy habits, they are a key part of living a successful life and maintaining a strong body. In the same way that negative words will drain your energy, promote stress and distract you from God's best; positive words will serve to restore your energy and promote joy and strength. Remember, positive words produce positive outcomes. Speak God's word and watch youthfulness be restored to your life.

Action Plan

STEP 1: Reveal – Have you ever paid attention to your words in the way you speak about your body and strength? What are some words that you have used in the past to define your physical body and strength?

_____

_____

_____

_____

STEP 2: Rethink – It is important to understand how powerful words are to the creation of your own self-image. Read and consider Psalms 139:14. Write what you believe that scripture is saying about you.

Psalms 139:14 - "I praise [thank] you because you made me in an amazing [awesome] and wonderful way. What you have done is wonderful. I know this very well." (NASB)

_____

_____

_____

_____

STEP 3: Replace – Now it's time to speak "good things". Write a few sentences as a personal declaration of who you are in your strength as a parent. It is a positive statement of your image as a parent, the strength you have in Christ and the image _He_ created within you. Take this statement and stand before a mirror and speak it over yourself. Do this daily. Watch your inner image grow stronger, more confident and yes, more youthful!

_____

_____

_____

_____

Prayer:

Thank you for how you created me and the transforming power of your Word.

Daily Declaration:

I have youthful strength. I speak good things which are positive and powerful words - God's words.

Joel 3:10 "... **_let the weak say, I am strong_**_"_ *(KJV)*

Communicate Strength

It is important to develop a community with other parents of children with special needs. It is through connections with others that you share ideas and gain information that can help you parent your child. This parent community can become a powerful platform for encouragement when everyone comes together with a mindset to empower one another with strength.

Receiving support during moments of weakness is a critical component of parenting. Joel 3:10 says, "let the weak say, I am strong". When those who are weak come together to create a dialogue focused on God's goodness, they begin to see more strength come into their lives. Sharing stories about the things God has done and the grace God has supplied for you to parent your child gives strength to those areas where you are weak. Regardless of what you may be feeling at the time, the more you focus on the Lord and His strength, the stronger you become.

In times of weakness, be mindful to surround yourself with conversations about God's strength. Be empowered by a collective exchange of supportive discussions. Let the weak say "I am strong"!

Action Plan

STEP 1: Re-examine - What conversations are you currently having with other parents of children with special needs? Are those communications promoting strength in your life?

_____

_____

_____

_____

STEP 2: Request – Allowing God to divinely connect you with other parents is essential to having an effective supportive community in your life. Take time in prayer and speak to God about the current status of your parent community. If you do not have community of parents in your life, talk to God about your desires in this area. Ask God to direct you to those individuals and organizations that can create the best community for you. Pray about participating with our partner organization, Encourage 365. It is a charitable organization that connects parents through an online community and empowerment sessions designed to encourage and strengthen parents of children with special needs. Visit encourage365.org.

STEP 3: Recognize - Identify ways in which God is leading you to develop and impact your parent community. If you are not currently engaged in a parent community, what are ways in which you can begin to connect with other parents for supportive discussions?

    1. _____

    2. _____

    3. _____

Prayer:

Lord, when I am weak, I say that I am strong. Help me to engage in conversation that supports and promotes the truth of your strength in my life. Lord thank you for opening doors for me to connect with other individuals and organizations that enhance your vision for my child and encourage me as a parent.

Daily Declaration:

Every day, I take hold of God's strength for my life. I am strong!

Joshua 1:7, "Only be strong and very courageous; be careful to do according to all the Law which Moses My servant commanded you; do not turn from it to the right or to the left, so that you may achieve success wherever you go" *(NASB)*

Dare to be Different

On the journey toward healing for your child, you may often find yourself pursuing different activities and treatment plans that are contrary to what the majority of other parents are doing. It may conflict with conventional thinking and the overall perspective of what "others" think you should do. No matter what steps you take, there is often this little voice that says, "You should just stop what you are doing", "Nobody else is doing it this way", "You're not going to be successful with this."

Finding the resolve to make decisions you believe are best for your child, even when other parents are doing something different, will take courage and strength. The story of Joshua gives a good example for us to follow. Joshua was called to take over land that was promised to him and his people. In facing this challenging task, God told Joshua, "[o]nly be strong and very courageous; be careful to do according to all the Law which Moses My servant commanded you; do not turn from it to the right or to the left, so that you may achieve success wherever you go." *(Joshua 1:7)*.

Success with decisions for your child will only come from following God as he leads and guides you. Especially if you are stepping out to do something different, it can only be done with the strength and courage given to you by God.

It is God's desire for His promises to be seen through you and your child. Seek God for his instructions and then pursue it. Dare to do what others are not willing to do. Dare to make adjustments when others are too afraid to move. Dare to make sacrifices other parents are not willing to make. Dare to walk in faith for your child, no matter what it looks like or what others have to say. Dare to be different!

Action Plan

STEP 1: Be Confident – Trusting God is a critical element of making decisions for your child. There will be times when God is leading you in a different direction than other parents. It may be something contrary to the typical treatment, method or regimen that others are using. To pursue what God is calling you to do, it will involve developing your confidence in the promises of God and His word. Read through Joshua 1:1-9. Read it repeatedly focusing on God's encouragement to Joshua for him to be strong and courageous and the promises of success God declared for Joshua. Then read it again, replacing Joshua's name with yours. Read it out loud saying your name in the context of the encouragement and promises God declares. The same words spoken to Joshua; God speaks to you also. Embrace it!

STEP 2: Be at Peace – Standing to be different does not mean you need to be aggressive. In fact, once you are confident in the way God is directing you, peace comes to your heart. You are able to proceed peacefully and lovingly with those who have differing opinions or positions. You are also able to share your perspectives with others in a more effective way. Take a moment to write out a prayer that you can say to yourself when you feel challenged with responding aggressively or when you are experiencing anxiety with speaking to others about your decision.

_____

_____

_____

_____

STEP 3: Be Convinced – Be willing to remain steadfast to what you believe is best for your child. Know that God is with you and willing to support you. You are not alone. His grace is there with you throughout the process.

Prayer:

God, I am open to your leadership. Guide me with making decisions for my child that will be in their best interest. Help me to communicate and express my decisions to others in a way that reflects your love, peace and goodness.

Daily Declaration:

I am strong and courageous. God directs me with the decisions I make. I am willing to be different whenever it is needed.

Ecclesiastes 4:9-10,12, "__Two are better than__ __one__, because they have a good return for their labor: __If either of them falls down, one can help__ __the other up__. But pity anyone who falls and has no one to help them up. __Though one may be__ __overpowered, two can defend themselves__." (NIV)

Strength in Numbers

Many parents feel alone in their journey of parenting a child who has been diagnosed with special needs. Facing the challenges by yourself can be very disheartening. To cope, some take on the attitude of "It's me and my child against the world!" – forging ahead by themselves trying to handle every aspect of their child's needs. Fortunately, God provides a better answer.

Standing alone in your parenting is not the best position. Instead, God wants to provide strength to you with the help of others. Ephesians 4:9-10,12 says "Two are better than one, . . . if either of them falls down, one can help the other up. . . Though one may be overpowered, two can defend themselves." Yes, there is strength in numbers.

There is no need to do everything alone. God gives you a team. Everyone from the medical staff that serves your child to the teachers at your child's school – these individuals represent a group that God has created to provide a helping hand. They are a part of the "team" God has provided for you. This "team" has the purpose of manifesting God's goodness and success for your child. Receive these individuals as part of your help. Embrace strength in numbers and never feel like you have to do it all by yourself.

Action Plan

STEP 1: Discover - It's time to find your team! Think about all the individuals you interact with concerning your child. It can be doctors, educators, therapists, family members and community groups. Take time to identify those individuals that are part of the "team" God has assembled to care for your child.

1._____   4._____

2._____   5._____

3._____   6._____

STEP 2: Intercede – Pray for your team. It is important to share love with those who are caring for your child. Praying for them creates an atmosphere where God's love and grace can be displayed through their interaction with you and your child.

STEP 3: Cooperate – Work with your team. Receive the help God has given you and then work together in peace to accomplish the goal of promoting success for your child. Consider it like "Game Time" where a sports team goes out together to accomplish the singular purpose of winning a game. You are going to receive help and work together with your "team" for the singular purpose of bringing forth God's best for your child. Remember, you are not alone. Use the team God has given you.

Prayer:

Lord, thank you that I am not alone. Thank you for the team that you provided. Teach me how to work with the individuals that are caring for my child in a way that demonstrates your love and promotes my child's success

Daily Declaration:

I receive the help God sends me. I have a Team that works together and we are achieving the goal of promoting success for my child.

Scripture Cards™

Each card is designed to be a quick reference to remind you of God's promises and help you stay encouraged. On the front is a scripture from each devotion in the book. On the back is a declaration to speak over your life. You can also write a personal message for what each scripture means to you. Cut out the cards to carry with you, post on your mirror or share with other parents.

*Numbers 13:30, "And Caleb stilled the people before Moses, and said, Let us go up at once, and possess it; **for we are well able to overcome it**"* (KJV

--- --- --- --- --- Cut Here --- --- --- --- ---

*Nehemiah 8:10, "**Go home and prepare a feast, holiday food and drink; and share it with those who don't have anything:** This day is holy to God. Don't feel bad. **The joy of God is your strength!**"* (MSG)

Declaration:

God's strength is operating in my life. I **AM** an overcomer!

What does <u>Numbers 13:30</u> mean to you?

_____

_____

_____

_____

_____

--- --- --- --- --- Cut Here --- --- --- --- ---

Declaration:

Today and every day, I walk in the joy of the Lord. I embrace joy and I share joy – for the joy of God is my strength.

What does <u>Nehemiah 8:10</u> mean to you?

_____

_____

_____

_____

_____

*Luke 6:38, "**Give and it shall be given unto you; good measure pressed down and shaken together, and running over shall men give into your bosom.** For with the same measure that you meet withal it shall be measured to you again."* (KJV)

--- --- --- --- --- Cut Here --- --- --- --- ---

*Philippians 4:13, "I can do **all things through Christ, who strengthens me**."* (EHV)

77

Declaration:

As I strengthen and encourage others, I too am strengthened and encouraged! I receive God's abundance of strength in good measure that is pressed down, shaken together and running over.

What does <u>Luke 6:38</u> mean to you?

_____

_____

_____

--- --- --- --- --- Cut Here --- --- --- --- ---

Declaration:

God's strength is greater than my own. I confront every challenge knowing that God's strength empowers me. Today and every day, I do all things through Christ who strengthens me.

What does <u>Philippians 4:13</u> mean to you?

_____

_____

_____

1John 4:4, *"But you belong to God, my dear children. **You have already won a victory** over those people, **because the Spirit who lives in you is greater than the spirit who lives in the world.**"* (NLT)

--- --- --- --- --- Cut Here --- --- --- --- ---

Ephesians 3:16, *"That He would grant you, according to the **riches of His glory** to be **strengthened with might** by His Spirit in the inner man."* (KJV)

79

Declaration:

God's strength within me is greater than anything outside of me. It is with his strength that I stand equipped and ready to have the victory over any challenge I face.

What does <u>1 John 4:4</u> mean to you?

_____

_____

_____

--- --- --- --- --- Cut Here --- --- --- --- ---

Declaration:

As I face this day, I am focused on God's "MIGHTY" strength given to me to address every situation and circumstance.

What does <u>Ephesians 3:16</u> mean to you?

_____

_____

_____

_____

_____

*Genesis 22:17, "That **in blessing I will bless thee, and in multiplying I will multiply thy seed** as the stars of heaven, and the sand which is upon the sea shore; and thy seed shall possess the gate of his enemies"* (KJV)

--- --- --- --- --- Cut Here --- --- --- --- ---

*3 John 2, " Beloved, I pray that in every way you may **succeed and prosper and be in good health [physically], just as [I know] your soul prospers [spiritually]**"* (AMP)

Declaration:

As I face this day, I am focused on God's "MIGHTY" strength given to me to address every situation and circumstance.

What does <u>Genesis 22:17</u> mean to you?

_____

_____

_____

_____

--- --- --- --- --- Cut Here --- --- --- --- ---

Declaration:

I prosper daily in my physical health. I receive God's wisdom and help to bring increased strength to every aspect of my body.

What does <u>3 John 2</u> mean to you?

_____

_____

_____

_____

_____

Proverbs 13:4, ".. .__the desires of the diligent are fully satisfied.__" (NIV)

--- --- --- --- --- Cut Here --- --- --- --- ---

Genesis 2:2, "And on the seventh day __God ended his work__ which he had made; __and he rested on the seventh day from all his work which he had made__." (KJV)

Declaration:

I stand today embracing God's love, diligently receiving his promises and moving forward for my child.

What does <u>Proverbs 13:4</u> mean to you?

_____

_____

_____

_____

--- --- --- --- --- Cut Here --- --- --- --- ---

Declaration:

I love who God made me to be and I purpose in my heart to get sufficient rest each day.

What does <u>Genesis 2:2</u> mean to you?

_____

_____

_____

_____

Psalm 103:5, "Who __satisfies your mouth with good things__; so that __your youth is renewed like eagles__" (NKJV)

--- --- --- --- --- Cut Here --- --- --- --- ---

Joel 3:10 ". . . __let the weak say, I am strong__" (KJV)

Declaration:

I have youthful strength. I speak good things which are positive and powerful words - God's words.

What does <u>Psalm 103:5</u> mean to you?

_____

_____

_____

_____

--- --- --- --- --- Cut Here --- --- --- --- ---

Declaration:

Every day, I take hold of God's strength for my life. I am strong!

What does <u>Joel 3:10</u> mean to you?

_____

_____

_____

_____

_____

Joshua 1:7, "Only be strong and very courageous; be careful to do according to all the Law which Moses My servant commanded you; do not turn from it to the right or to the left, so that you may achieve success wherever you go" *(NASB)*

--- --- --- --- --- --- Cut Here --- --- --- --- --- ---

Ecclesiastes 4:9-10,12, "**Two are better than one**, *because they have a good return for their labor:* **If either of them falls down, one can help the other up**. *But pity anyone who falls and has no one to help them up.* **Though one may be overpowered, two can defend themselves**." *(NIV)*

Declaration:

I am strong and courageous. God directs me with the decisions I make. I am willing to be different whenever it is needed.

What does <u>Joshua 1:7</u> mean to you?

_____

_____

_____

_____

--- --- --- --- --- Cut Here --- --- --- --- ---

Declaration:

I receive the help God sends me. I have a Team that works together and we are achieving the goal of promoting success for my child.

What does <u>Ecclesiastes 4:9-10,12</u> mean to you?

_____

_____

_____

_____

Share Your Story

We want to hear from you! Give us your testimony of how this book has helped you. Share your encouragement victories with us. Visit our website www.encouragedevotions.com.

Empowerment Sessions

Receive inspiration, get equipped and be supported through live and recorded sessions where we talk through each devotion and discuss practical steps to put your action plan to work. These "Empowerment Sessions" are designed to provide additional insight and create a time of encouragement for parents who may be struggling. Visit the website of our partner Encourage 365, Inc. (a non-profit, charitable organization) at www.encourage365.org to sign up and participate.

90

About the Author

Janis C Jones is the mother of a child diagnosed with special needs. Throughout her parenting journey, she faced issues of isolation, fear, abandonment and disappointment. It was through her faith in God's word that she was able to find encouragement to press forward and believe the best for her child's future. The scripture in Psalm 27:13 best describes her experience.

I would have fainted, unless I had believed that I would see the goodness of the LORD in the land of the living. (KJ)

Sharing the word of God to encourage parents of children with special needs is her passion. As a former attorney, she refocused her career to become an author, speaker and empowerment leader creating devotional books and content that encourages and uplifts. She is available to speak with your group, church, school, organization or business to share the message of encouragement. Feel free to connect with her on social media and visit her website to schedule a speaking engagement. www.janiscjones.com.